# POETRY Wonderland

## Poets From Buckinghamshire

Edited By Lindsay Joyce

First published in Great Britain in 2019 by:

**Young Writers**
Est. 1991

Young Writers
Remus House
Coltsfoot Drive
Peterborough
PE2 9BF
Telephone: 01733 890066
Website: www.youngwriters.co.uk

All Rights Reserved
Book Design by Ashley Janson
© Copyright Contributors 2019
SB ISBN 978-1-78988-195-0
Printed and bound in the UK by BookPrintingUK
Website: www.bookprintinguk.com
YB0392A

# FOREWORD

Here at Young Writers, we love to let imaginations run wild and creativity go crazy. Our aim is to encourage young people to get their creative juices flowing and put pen to paper. Each competition is tailored to the relevant age group, hopefully giving each pupil the inspiration and incentive to create their own piece of creative writing, whether it's a poem or a short story. By allowing them to see their own work in print, we know their confidence and love for the written word will grow.

For our latest competition Poetry Wonderland, we invited primary school pupils to create wild and wonderful poems on any topic they liked – the only limits were the limits of their imagination! Using poetry as their magic wand, these young poets have conjured up worlds, creatures and situations that will amaze and astound or scare and startle! Using a variety of poetic forms of their own choosing, they have allowed us to get a glimpse into their vivid imaginations. We hope you enjoy wandering through the wonders of this book as much as we have.

# CONTENTS

**Akeley Wood Junior School, Wicken**

| | |
|---|---|
| Naomi Evelyn Parrott (10) | 1 |
| Sam Yardley (10) | 2 |
| Annabel Wheble (10) | 4 |
| Laura Rosenberg (10) | 6 |
| Crawford Jacobs (9) | 7 |
| Connor Lyne (9) | 8 |
| Isaac Geudon (10) | 10 |
| Izzy Cruickshank (7) | 11 |
| Lewis Andrew Wilson (7) | 12 |
| Harrison Evans (9) | 13 |
| Lainey Frahm (8) | 14 |
| Georgie Ledger (9) | 15 |
| Samuel Korede Ajakaye (10) | 16 |
| Harry Ewings (9) | 18 |
| Samuel Jones (9) | 19 |
| Henry Plested (9) | 20 |
| Emma Swain (7) | 21 |
| George Martin McEntee (8) | 22 |
| Reece Evans (9) | 23 |
| Archie German (9) | 24 |
| Michaela Heim (9) | 25 |
| Isabelle Wadsworth (8) | 26 |
| Tate Archer (9) | 27 |
| Isabel Rose Butterworth (10) | 28 |
| Toby Hayward (9) | 29 |
| Harry Smith | 30 |
| Hunter | 31 |
| Erin-Mae Hobbs (9) | 32 |
| Oli Theodoulou | 33 |
| Sebastian Shipstone (9) | 34 |
| Liam James Williamson (8) | 35 |

**Brooklands Farm Primary School, Milton Keynes**

| | |
|---|---|
| Maryam Akintayo (11) | 36 |
| Lakshith Dasari (9) | 38 |
| Loriana Kalou (10) | 40 |
| Salmo Hussein (10) | 42 |
| Skye Welsh (10) | 44 |
| Gyasi Mensah (8) | 46 |
| Kasey Taylor (10) | 48 |
| Henry Stoney (9) | 50 |
| Irene Tolosa Zambrano (8) | 52 |
| Alfie Taylor (9) | 54 |
| Nicolo Testa (8) | 56 |
| Ilze Pociute (8) | 58 |
| Nikolas Jovanovic (8) | 60 |
| Freddie James Haywood (8) | 62 |
| Alfie Hirst (9) | 64 |
| Alex Waller (9) | 66 |
| Emily Short (9) | 68 |
| Emilie Higgs (8) | 69 |
| Em-Jaye Goddphin (10) | 70 |
| Rehan Khokhar (9) | 72 |
| Amelia Mustafa (10) | 74 |
| Sarina Lawrence (8) | 76 |
| Kiera Whitham (8) | 77 |
| Julie Ann Donbeinaa (9) | 78 |
| Miami Maddison John (8) | 79 |
| Rupert Vibush Sripathy (8) | 80 |
| Priscilla Otchere (10) | 82 |
| Lichelle Schumachers (9) | 84 |
| Jeffrey Kacou (8) | 86 |
| Jaime Gomez (8) | 87 |
| Lina El-Majdki (9) | 88 |
| Mia Rose Stevens (9) | 89 |
| Amberley Chikukwa (11) | 90 |

| | |
|---|---|
| Aya Houria Mouhi (10) | 92 |
| Anna Kotyza (8) | 93 |
| Ellie Patricia Keeble (9) | 94 |
| Anna Ungureanu (10) | 95 |
| Ridhima Das (8) | 96 |
| Ryan Coppin (10) | 97 |
| Nathaniel James Wood (9) | 98 |
| Wiktoria Ostrowska (9) | 100 |
| Mina Fatima (9) | 101 |
| Stephen Lam (8) | 102 |
| Olivia Sparrow (9) | 103 |
| Liam Arslan (7) | 104 |
| Tyson Romeo John (10) | 105 |
| Leah Quigley (7) | 106 |
| Maher Parikh (8) | 107 |
| Marley Steven Maison (7) | 108 |
| Millie Marjorie Germain (7) | 109 |
| Toni Akinsanya (7) | 110 |
| Pahal Patel (7) | 111 |
| Daisey Adams (8) | 112 |
| Kieran Peter Allwood (8) | 113 |
| Sanah Kumar (7) | 114 |
| Riley Childs (8) | 115 |
| Mugdha Gowri Basanth (7) | 116 |
| Layla Sharman (7) | 117 |
| Ella Sparrow (7) | 118 |
| Ewan George Roberts (8) | 119 |
| Pranav Gupta (7) | 120 |
| Kailen Helm (8) | 121 |
| Lillie-Mae Weller (7) | 122 |
| Aimee Joy Haggis (7) | 123 |
| Taimaa Al Haj Ali (7) | 124 |
| Borys Sawicki (7) | 125 |
| Anya Reddy (7) | 126 |
| Kiara Patel (7) | 127 |
| Calum O'Sullivan (8) | 128 |
| Jayden Lau (7) | 129 |
| Leah Mae Wears (7) | 130 |
| Karishma Patel (7) | 131 |

## Haddenham Community Junior School, Haddenham

| | |
|---|---|
| Rivkah Richards-Gray (9) | 132 |

## Millbrook Combined School, High Wycombe

| | |
|---|---|
| Salah-Udeen Nabi (9) | 133 |
| Mimi Burrough (10) | 134 |
| Ramisa Hussain (10) | 136 |
| Jason Frimpong (9) | 138 |
| Sophie Weston (9) | 140 |
| Senthur Senthilnathan (10) | 142 |
| Millie Zena Pearce (9) | 143 |
| Emilia Czech (11) | 144 |
| Aryan (10) | 146 |
| Stefania Valentina Pantazi (10) | 147 |
| Hassan Bin Suleman Hussain (10) | 148 |
| Mia Lashbrook (10) | 149 |
| Faiqa Khan (9) | 150 |
| Umair Hussain (10) | 151 |
| Maryam Fakraz (9) | 152 |
| Michal Zablocki (9) | 153 |
| Tanvi Ramkissoom (9) | 154 |
| Jamilia Korb (9) | 155 |
| Spencer Humphreys (10) | 156 |
| George Risness (9) | 157 |
| Nithuja Jegan (9) | 158 |
| Zaeem Ghauri (9) | 159 |
| Bazagh (10) | 160 |
| Barakaath Bashir (9) | 161 |
| Alexandra Dorina Sutic (10) | 162 |
| Amelia Hussain (9) | 163 |
| Isabelle Alexander (9) | 164 |
| Saif Ayub (9) | 165 |
| Aleesha Saba (10) | 166 |
| Manahil Javed (10) | 167 |
| Harvey Richards (9) | 168 |
| Ameera Amer (9) | 169 |
| Debby Adeorike Lawal (10) | 170 |
| Indumini Wijerathne (9) | 171 |
| Thalia Sehmbi (9) | 172 |

| | |
|---|---|
| Sandra Mihaela Stoica (9) | 173 |
| Zara Masood (10) | 174 |
| Nana-Yaa Sarpong (9) | 175 |
| Harrison Blackwell (10) | 176 |
| Hafsah Zaman (9) | 177 |
| Adam Kharbouch (9) | 178 |
| Oskar Poprawa (9) | 179 |
| Hannan Hussain (9) | 180 |
| Namra Mahmood (9) | 181 |
| Hashim Asim (10) | 182 |
| Mohammed Ali Mehmood | 183 |
| Dylan Olando Derby (9) | 184 |
| Archie Julian Jeffries (11) | 185 |

### Woodside Junior School, Amersham

| | |
|---|---|
| Anushree Nikhil Kaluskar (10) | 186 |
| Mattis Cook (8) | 187 |
| Rosie Horton (10) | 188 |
| Isabel Hibberd (10) | 189 |
| Kimberley Revel (9) | 190 |
| Ajooni Jassy (10) | 191 |
| Dixie Ferguson (9) | 192 |
| Becky Kemp (7) | 193 |
| Lehna Kaur Bains (9) | 194 |
| Molly Meehan (7) | 195 |
| Elasia Kate Jbilou (7) | 196 |

# ★ The Poems ★

# The Cookie Revolution

I just came back from holiday,
it was a lovely day in May.
A man started kissing the ground,
he said, "It tasted like cookie dough!"

I thought *that can't be true*,
but the Cookie Revolution was something nobody knew.
Out of the blue, I heard a sound,
It sounded like an earthquake shaking the ground.

But nobody knew that the world was going flat,
the Cookie Revolution's rain came down with a splat!
In two days, a boat sailed off the edge,
and I saw it from a ledge!

By then, I knew the world was a cookie,
the Cookie Revolution has now spread to a place called Wookey!
Now I feel cookie dough at the beach,
people are saying 'so long!' to the peach!

**Naomi Evelyn Parrott (10)**
Akeley Wood Junior School, Wicken

# A Sweet Adventure In Space

One day, I looked up to the sky
And wondered what it would be like to fly
A rocket ship to the moon
I don't think I'd get there soon
First, I'd surf the Milky Way
And going to Mars would take a day
A boost would make my ship go fast
I'd make that galaxy at last
As my ship twirled past Jupiter and Uranus
I thought of stopping off at Venus
I landed with a thump and fell into a crater full of green gel
Suddenly, there were aliens around
I didn't dare to breathe or make a sound
The aliens were excited at what they saw
They turned the handle and opened the door
I knew I had to make friends quick
What could I give them, what could I pick?
How about my very last Twix?

In return, they could help me fix
My broken ship and get me home
To put my feet up with a Toblerone.

**Sam Yardley (10)**
Akeley Wood Junior School, Wicken

# Imagine Human Dogs

I open my eyes
And see the most amazing creatures
Staring back at me with big, adoring eyes.

Furry, fluffy legs of dogs,
Blending into humans' hands and heads,
Confused but excited, I look around in wonder,
As they run and jump around playfully.

Their fluff and fur and a cold wet nose,
The soft tickling fur that mats,
When it's not brushed and cared for.

I speak to say hello,
And yet a soft bark comes out of my mouth,
I am speaking the language Doggish.

The human dogs greet me,
With excited barks and endearing nose nuzzles,
Long tails wagging.

The endless love a dog gives,
The kisses, the cuddles, the licks,
That make me laugh and make me happy.

I never want or need to close my eyes again,
No need to escape where I am,
This is me.

## Annabel Wheble (10)
Akeley Wood Junior School, Wicken

# Planet Jump

In my dreams, I like to jump from one planet to another.
On this journey, I'd like to take my brother.

We started on Mercury, which is the closest to the sun.
Oh, it's really hot, we need to run.

We jumped to Venus, which shines really strong.
Without your sunglasses, you make something wrong.

The next planet is Earth, where we live all together.
And we are always happy when we have nice weather.

Now we jumped to the red planet, Mars.
And, from there, we can see shiny stars.

Now we are on Jupiter, it's the biggest planet circling around our sun.
And on this stony surface, you can have a lot of fun.

**Laura Rosenberg (10)**
Akeley Wood Junior School, Wicken

# Meteor Ride

This meteor I'm on,
I have to say
It's a lot of fun.
Seeing all the stars flying by
And the tail kind of looks like a butterfly.
"Wait!" I cried.
That's when I noticed my butt being fried,
Quick, I need to get off.
I jumped and saw a spaceship,
"Help! I'm floating off!"
They saved me in time,
Because I was going to
turn into a squashed lime.
Wow, Earth looks so
Tiny from here or maybe
I'm just so weeny.
I hope my family does
Miss me because I miss
them massively now.
I've run out of time,
I guess this is the end of my rhymes.

## Crawford Jacobs (9)
Akeley Wood Junior School, Wicken

# Convincing The Sun Not To Shine

Once upon a time,
I tried to convince the sun not to shine.
My maths exam was in two days,
I was thinking of lots of ways,
secretly hoping my teachers had forgot,
otherwise, I'd be getting a big red dot.
Suddenly, I had it,
I put on my space kit,
and off I went to try and
convince the sun to rest for a bit.
I begged and pleaded,
I lied and I cried,
I asked him to stay away,
Just for one exam day!
He didn't say a word,
I thought that was a bit absurd.
Off I went home to bed,
filled with dread.

Now I sit here,
no maths in my head.
Gosh! I wish I'd studied a bit!

## Connor Lyne (9)
Akeley Wood Junior School, Wicken

# Dinosaur Planet

**D** inosaurs still exist you know,
**I** don't mean here on Earth though.
**N** ow I was reliably told,
**O** f a planet made of gold.
**S** tegasauruses the size of a speck,
**A** nkylosaurus that are a pain in the neck.
**U** tahraptors you can barely see,
**R** eptiles simply roaming free.

**P** lanet Jurassic is actually tiny,
**L** ost in space even though it's shiny.
**A** liens shrunk them to collect,
**N** ano versions to inspect.
**E** very species there's ever been,
**T** ogether on a golden tangerine.

**Isaac Geudon (10)**
Akeley Wood Junior School, Wicken

# Magic Key

Magic Key, so elegant and nice
I would touch you but I have lice,
My brother used to be slick,
But now he is thick,
So you can bear that in mind,
If you want to spy,
On him in his room,
You can do it in light, the full moon.
You are beautiful,
Not like an ugly bull,
I will treasure you forever,
Just like a priceless feather.
You will be able to produce lots of light,
In the full moon tonight,
Because I will help you,
To be helpful.
In the full moon tonight.

**Izzy Cruickshank (7)**
Akeley Wood Junior School, Wicken

# My Flying Pig

**M** y flying pig has beautiful purple and pink wings
**Y** our pig is as dull as anything

**F** ly pig fly!
**L** ovely girl, steady on by!
**Y** o! Down there, what are you doing to my house?
**I** 'm doing graffiti on it you ugly mouse!
**N** oooo!
**G** o and get him piggy.

**P** hew! He knocked him out easy peasy
**I** won... wait a minute
**G** olly gosh I'm so stupid, this is graffiti piggy land. Now the piggy will go to jail.

**Lewis Andrew Wilson (7)**
Akeley Wood Junior School, Wicken

# Hamburger World

     **H** i, I'm Harrison an astronaut!
     **A** nd I'm on a planet called Hamburger,
     **M** y goodness where to start, ah yes there are
     **B** urger aliens, tomato bombs, cheese cannons
Yo **U** should really see it's really, really exciting.
     **R** ight, when you eat a burger at midnight,
     **G** o to the window and you will just see it!
     **E** r, a ketchup sea, lettuce trees and burger buildings,
     **R** ight, that's it, give me a big round of applause, yay!

## Harrison Evans (9)
Akeley Wood Junior School, Wicken

# Cloud Castle

Riding on my fluffy, flying dog,
towering over the pink birds, the fierce dragons,
and the flying unicorns.
Riding in the sky to my magical cloud castle
through the whipping wind, past the sparkling clouds.
I fly forward to the fire-breathing dragon,
and I watch the sparkly, pink birds fly past me.
The cloud village fades,
and I'm finally there,
past the pink, sparkling birds,
past the sparkling clouds,
dancing in my shimmering, sparkling castle.

**Lainey Frahm (8)**
Akeley Wood Junior School, Wicken

# Up In Space

I live in space
That's a whole different case
As I glide through the air
I have more time to spare
I see coloured balloons up high
Up above the gigantic blue sky
As I look at the planets
I began to hear a racket
I look above and I see a rocket
I had to be honest
They didn't lock it!
As it comes rushing down
It falls crashing on the town.

**Georgie Ledger (9)**
Akeley Wood Junior School, Wicken

# Out Of The Blue

Out of the blue
I saw you
My best friend
On the loo

Out of the blue
I saw some mice
So I was nice and said
"Do you want some rice?"

Out of the blue
I saw ice
Cold as ice cream
But still as nice

Out of the blue
Was Winnie The Pooh
With Christopher Robin
And all of his crew

Out of the blue
I saw you

I'm back to normal
And so are you

## Samuel Korede Ajakaye (10)
Akeley Wood Junior School, Wicken

# Living In A Cactus

Living in a cactus,
So boring nothing to do,
No space to sleep.
"Help! Help!"
Being attacked by birds as vicious as lions,
Phew! I'm well protected by the spikes,
My back is itchy with bumpy stems.
I see a coconut tree in the distance,
No water in sight.
Sand flying into my mouth,
I'm trying to spit it out,
I can hear wind,
*Whoosh, whoosh, whoosh!*

**Harry Ewings (9)**
Akeley Wood Junior School, Wicken

# Amazing Asteroids

- **A** steroids flying through the air
- **S** olar system
- **T** winkling stars
- **E** xplode in a bright supernova
- **R** ockets blast off into space
- **O** rbiting the moon
- **I** nventions like telescopes looking into space
- **D** azzling planets we can see
- **S** aturn, Mercury, Jupiter, Mars, and Venus all named after the Roman Gods.

## Samuel Jones (9)
Akeley Wood Junior School, Wicken

# Living In A Pencil

I open my eyes it's quiet and still
I've been in my case all night having a chill.
The noise has started
Living in a pencil is not for the faint-hearted.
I feel so dizzy, I'm working so hard
Learning new words for friends' birthday cards.
I now know more stuff and I am very tired
How will I sleep tonight? I'm still totally wired!

**Henry Plested (9)**
Akeley Wood Junior School, Wicken

# Naked Bear

**S** illy old bear
**H** air all tatty and worn
**A** lways looking messy
**V** ery soft to cuddle
**E** veryone's favourite friend.

**A** little bit cheeky.

**B** ut never looking his best
**E** arly one morning time for a change
**A** ll tatty hair has gone in one minute
**R** emoved by a shaver.

## Emma Swain (7)
Akeley Wood Junior School, Wicken

# Submarine Wonderland

I am a chocolate submarine flying in the air,
It is Submarine Wonderland
Oh, it's so beautifully fair.
In my country, I am cool and everyone else rules.
I go to this shop called Tesco
And the only thing I buy is related to my friend Franchesco!
My house is so cool
Because it has its own floating swimming pool!

### George Martin McEntee (8)
Akeley Wood Junior School, Wicken

# My Lego Came Alive

My Lego came to life,
it whizzed through the air.
What a miniature surprise!

I hear the birds tweeting,
is my Lego hedgehog coming to life?
Colourful shapes, big and small,
there's my Lego hedgehog kicking a ball.

I feel happy now my hedgehog is alive.
Now let's go and build a baby monkey to bring to life.

**Reece Evans (9)**
Akeley Wood Junior School, Wicken

# My Meteorite

I am riding a meteor
Which is super dumb,
But super fun!
I am riding my meteorite,
Whilst flying my kite.
Oh, I see something.
Maybe an alien?
What? A potato?
Now I'm through a black hole,
With my comb, styling my hair.
Still on my meteorite in another dimension,
An invention dimension.

**Archie German (9)**
Akeley Wood Junior School, Wicken

# Mars Village

**V** illage of many mysterious creatures
**I** nteresting and dangerous
**L** ocated in red-hot Mars
**L** oud dragons breathe red hot fire
**A** boiling red hot lava castle
**G** iant with red creepy eyes
**E** lves of the bright lava falls.

**Michaela Heim (9)**
Akeley Wood Junior School, Wicken

# Antvengers

Ants, ants in lots of history
When were they found is such a mystery
When were they seen
In their big house-bean
No one knew more
Than what they saw
The Antvengers were defenders
And the humans know now the ants' adventures!

**Isabelle Wadsworth (8)**
Akeley Wood Junior School, Wicken

# Planet

I wonder what it would be like.
Being a planet all alone, doing nothing.
I wonder what it would be like
Having no friends or having a house to live in.
Just sat there far away from Earth
Watching everyone have fun?

## Tate Archer (9)
Akeley Wood Junior School, Wicken

# Amazing Food

Great British Bake Off tent,
Creative, yummy
Observing, judging, baking
Everyone making, baking quick.
Exhausting!

**Isabel Rose Butterworth (10)**
Akeley Wood Junior School, Wicken

# The Tower Of London

The Tower of London
Ancient, royal
Defending, guarding, protecting
A popular tourist attraction
Overwhelmed.

**Toby Hayward (9)**
Akeley Wood Junior School, Wicken

# Val Thorens

Val Thorens
Snowy, cold
Skiing, snowboarding, ice dancing
Avalanche made by skiers
Scared.

**Harry Smith**
Akeley Wood Junior School, Wicken

# Hunter's Treehouse

Rustic, playground.
Sleeping, zip wiring, creating.
My special secret hideaway.
Happy.

**Hunter**
Akeley Wood Junior School, Wicken

# Bella My Dog

Bella
Fluffy, cuddly
Munching, swimming, sprinting
My adorable best friend
Safe.

## Erin-Mae Hobbs (9)
Akeley Wood Junior School, Wicken

# The Alps

The Alps
Massive, snowy
Skiing, racing, watching
Steep white smooth slopes
Alive!

**Oli Theodoulou**
Akeley Wood Junior School, Wicken

# Florida

Sun, thrills
Riding, sliding, playing
Sunny playground of fun
Happy.

## Sebastian Shipstone (9)
Akeley Wood Junior School, Wicken

# London Eye

Big, wheel
Turning, viewing, pointing
Lots of people inside
High.

**Liam James Williamson (8)**
Akeley Wood Junior School, Wicken

# The Circle Of School

We start school when were four
Most of us will find it a bore
We snore
We sleep on the floor
A few hours later we do even more.

One year later...
We're finally in Year One
And we feel much greater
Now we are learning all about determination
This is fun I'm very certain
We never give up on what Miss Rose taught us
She also tells us never to fuss.

One year later...
We're in Year Two
Now we are calm
Our colour is blue
Mrs Taylor always tells us to stay calm
Especially the boy in my class named Tom.

One year later...
I'm learning about balance

We're finally upstairs
Now that we are in Key Stage Two
Key Stage One for me is currently invalid
We are starting to be more independent
Those two year groups are very different.

One year later...
I'm in Year Four
We're learning about achievements
My teacher name is Miss Gilders
You'll never forget her
No offence to your teacher
But she's probably better.

One year later...
I'm in Year Five
She is extremely kind
Her names Miss Downey
She'll probably even give me a brownie.

Now I'm in Year Six
I've only just started
There is a lot more to come
Don't let us get departed.

## Maryam Akintayo (11)
Brooklands Farm Primary School, Milton Keynes

# Becoming Into An Individual

Be in the world you want to see,
An individual you want to be.
Be in the land you always dreamed,
I wonder why I'd be a meme.
Listen to me it's the key,
Then go home and drink some tea.
Listen to me, don't be a meme,
Then go home and listen to a theme.

I work independently in my home
While I do it with a happy tone.
I finish it quickly all alone,
Why should I do it with a moan.
Tell me, tell me if you're sad
Then I'll sort you with a hand.
Tell me, tell me if you're mad
Then I'll sort you in your land.

Please show no ungrateful manners
And don't be an annoying chatter.

Please show no ungrateful matters
But I won't listen with your chatter.
Don't get involved with my matter
And don't even listen to my chatter.
Don't get involved with my matter
And I won't get involved with your matter.

Back in the past, I was in Year Four,
But I don't know why I want some more.
Back in the past, I was in Year Four,
Now I'll tell you why I want some more.
Right now, I'm in Year Five,
So I become an individual
And have a great life.
Right now, I'm in Year Five,
So I can become an individual
And now, I'm all mine.

## Lakshith Dasari (9)
Brooklands Farm Primary School, Milton Keynes

# Change

In Year One, I had some fun,
I played all day until I was done.
I learned to count all the way to fifty,
And I must say, I was pretty shifty.
I had my favourite teddy bear,
And I must say, it had lots of hair.

In Year Two, I had a nice teacher,
I must add, she had beautiful features.
Her blonde hair shone in the sun,
As we played one by one.

In Year Three, we played on trees,
As we felt the warm hot breeze.
If I remember, we did some swimming,
And also helped the teachers with trimming.

In Year Four, it was so much fun,
For we had so many things to be done.
For example, the Greek ignite day,
We also had time to have a big play.
We also had a big pizza,
I must point out it was a Greek one!

In Year Five, Mr Kerin was a blast,
And he ran really fast!
We also went to the park to play,
Also, it was a very sunny day!
We skipped and played all day long,
And we felt pretty strong.

Now I'm in Year Six.
Lots to learn and things to turn.
Soon I am going to have my SATs!
Argh! There are rats!

## Loriana Kalou (10)
Brooklands Farm Primary School, Milton Keynes

# Change

I don't really remember Year One
But I knew I was the tallest,
And I knew it was fun.
I played on the climbing frame all day,
One thing I normally did was play.

It was better in Year Two,
We went to the theatre,
You should've come too.
We watched a movie with popcorn and food,
One time, we had pancakes,
And they tasted good!

I joined a new school when I was in Year Three,
I learned about chucking,
I was impressed by me,
I also met a teacher called My Gray.
I really wanted him to stay.

By now, I'm onto Year Four,
I had special classes,
But not anymore.

Then we went to do some swimming,
I was really bad, but I felt like winning.

Yay, we're in Year Five,
We are now individual and more alive!
We got to watch Harry Potter,
We had Mr Kerin and he isn't a rotter.

Finally, we're in Year Six,
We now have an LZ to fix.
I am now going to start making friends.
We will stay friends until primary school ends.

## Salmo Hussein (10)
Brooklands Farm Primary School, Milton Keynes

# My Change At School

In Year One
I learned my ABCs
And then, for lunch
We had sandwiches and cheese.

In Year Two
The teachers were nice
They were ever so clever
And they gave me great advice.

In Year Three
We learned sex education
It was quite interesting
But people shouted out in exclamation.

In Year Four
Maths was hard
I ought to give myself
A big sympathy card.

In Year Five
We learned about space

And wow that subject
Was such a showcase.

In Year Six
I loved school
When I came here
Everyone was cool.

Here I am
Here is my change
And I don't find this school
The least bit strange

Strong and powerful
Are our words
Here is a fact about me
I hate lemon curd.

Now I have three important words
Roll up your red sleeves
Ready to hear them?
They are 'Open, Grow and Believe!'

## Skye Welsh (10)
Brooklands Farm Primary School, Milton Keynes

# If I Were In Charge Of The World

If I were in charge of the world,
I'd cancel school detentions, bullies, mean teachers and also nightmares.

If I were in charge of the world,
there'd be 10 billion pounds once a week,
free McDonald's,
and disaster-proof houses.

If I were in charge of the world,
you wouldn't have presidents,
you wouldn't have poor people,
you wouldn't have sisters or hear "Don't punch your brother!"
and you wouldn't even have schools you sleep at.

If I were in charge of the world,
McDonald's, KFC, sweets, and Domino's would be a vegetable.
All 18 games and movies would be PG

and a person who sometimes forgets to brush their teeth
and sometimes forgets to get to sleep early
would still be allowed to be in charge of the world!

## Gyasi Mensah (8)
Brooklands Farm Primary School, Milton Keynes

# Always Change

In Year One, I loved to cuddle
A little bear I named Buddle
I still have it to this day
I will never get taken away
I learned the alphabet off by heart
Until I made a bigger start.

In Year Two, I drew
A picture of my mum
Whilst my friend played the drum.

In Year Three, I disagreed
With everything I was told
I would always be cold.

In Year Four, I learned to roar
Along with my friends
We would follow the trend.

In Year Five, I had to survive
With all the boys
They made lots of noise.

In Year Six, I'm learning the basics
Still not ready for Year Seven
I hope that it's heaven.

Moved to this school
It's ever so cool
We stick to three words
'Open, Grow, Believe.'

## Kasey Taylor (10)
Brooklands Farm Primary School, Milton Keynes

# If I Were In Charge Of The World

If I were in charge of the world,
I'd cancel Fortnite, pink, girls
and also Donald Trump.

If I were in charge of the world,
There'd be Alex as a prince,
girls would be boys,
Harry Potter people
and I would be king of the world.

If I were in charge of the world,
You wouldn't have literacy,
You wouldn't have Brexit,
You wouldn't have paper,
You wouldn't have pencils.
You wouldn't even have colourful ones.

If I were in charge of the world a gigantic,
chocolatey, caramelly fudge ice cream sundae
would be a vegetable,
all films would be PG

and a person who sometimes forgets to eat
and sometimes forgets to drink
would still be allowed to be in charge of the world.

## Henry Stoney (9)
Brooklands Farm Primary School, Milton Keynes

# If I Were In Charge Of The World

If I were in charge of the world,
I'd cancel killing animals,
eating too many sweets,
plastic bottles in the sea
and also spiders.

If I were in charge of the world,
there be unicorns and fairies,
you live forever and you'd fly like a unicorn.

If I were in charge of the world,
You wouldn't have smoking,
You wouldn't have to get old,
You wouldn't have too many toys,
Or stuff that you don't use.
You would even have flying puppies.

If I were in charge of the world,
Lots of sweets would be a vegetable,
All spiders would be harmless,

And a person who forgets to brush their teeth
And sometimes forgets to wash
Would still be allowed to be in charge of the world.

## Irene Tolosa Zambrano (8)
Brooklands Farm Primary School, Milton Keynes

# If I Were In Charge Of The World

If I were in charge of the world,
I'd cancel detentions,
manual doors,
manual blinds
and also scary movies.

If I were in charge of the world,
there'd be really, really good police
who always catch the robbers,
real cars for kids
and double presents for Christmas and birthdays.

If I were in charge of the world,
you wouldn't have school,
you wouldn't have wasps,
you wouldn't have Papa Johns
and you wouldn't have allergies.

If I were in charge of the world,
large pizza would be a vegetable,
all doors would be automatic

and a person who forgets to have lunch
and sometimes forget to bath
would still be allowed to be in charge of the world!

## Alfie Taylor (9)
Brooklands Farm Primary School, Milton Keynes

# If I Were In Charge Of The World

If I were in charge of the world,
I'd cancel murderers,
Monday afternoons,
After school clubs and also injections.

If I were in charge of the world,
There'd be immortality,
Real emojis,
And you would get five pom-poms at a time.

If I were in charge of the world,
You wouldn't have easy passwords,
You wouldn't have primary colours,
You wouldn't have uncomfy cushions,
You wouldn't pay the shopkeepers!
You wouldn't even have shopkeepers.

If I were in charge of the world,
Ice cream would be a veg,
All movie age ratings would be halved

And a person who forgets to sleep
And forgets to eat
Would still be allowed to be in charge of the world.

## Nicolo Testa (8)
Brooklands Farm Primary School, Milton Keynes

# If I Were In Charge Of The World

If I were in charge of the world,
I'd cancel killing, wars, fighting
and also rainy days.

If I were in charge of the world,
there'd be fairies, unicorns
and everyone could choose
what age they wanted to be.

If I were in charge of the world,
you wouldn't have annoying people,
you wouldn't have peppers,
you wouldn't have smoking or sleeping,
you wouldn't even have bedtimes.

If I were in charge of the world,
vanilla and bubblegum ice cream
would be a vegetable,
all dinosaurs would not be evil
and a person who sometimes
forgets to read a story

and sometimes forgets to eat chocolate
would still be allowed to be in charge of the world.

## Ilze Pociute (8)
Brooklands Farm Primary School, Milton Keynes

# If I Were In Charge Of The World

If I were in charge of the world,
I'd cancel adults, schools, books,
sickness, and principles.

If I were in charge of the world,
there'd be paradise,
every electronic device would be free.

If I were in charge of the world,
you wouldn't have haters,
you wouldn't have annoying brothers,
you wouldn't have guns or hear "Don't go to sleep!"
and wouldn't even have beds.

If I were in charge of the world,
ice cream with strawberry sauce
would be a vegetable
and also a plain biscuit
and a person who sometimes
forgets to get changed

and sometimes forgets to brush their teeth
would still be allowed to be in charge of the world.

## Nikolas Jovanovic (8)
Brooklands Farm Primary School, Milton Keynes

# If I Were In Charge Of The World

If I were in charge of the world,
I'd cancel school, natural disasters, bullies
and also detentions.

If I were in charge of the world,
there'd be £12 once a week,
no deaths
and lots of *bananas!*

If I were in charge of the world,
you wouldn't have any names,
you wouldn't have homework,
you wouldn't have buses
and you wouldn't have warnings
about punching your brother.

If I were in charge of the world,
KFC would be a vegetable,
we would live for millions of years
and a person who sometimes
forgets to brush his teeth

and sometimes forgets to flush
would still be allowed to be in charge of the world!

## Freddie James Haywood (8)
Brooklands Farm Primary School, Milton Keynes

# If I Were In Charge Of The World

If I were in charge of the world,
I'd cancel vegetables,
Wednesday mornings,
pins and needles
and also Harry Styles.

If I were in charge of the world,
there'd be no nightlights,
I'd heal all animals
and football goals would be 200 inches bigger.

If I were in charge of the world,
you wouldn't be sad,
you wouldn't be dirty,
you wouldn't have a bedtime or even have cows.

If I were in charge of the world,
a game called Fortnite would rule.
White chocolate would be a vegetable,
all adult movies would be PG
and a person who forgets to wash

or sometimes forgets to flush
would still be in charge of the world!

## Alfie Hirst (9)
Brooklands Farm Primary School, Milton Keynes

# Becoming An Individual

Individual is my word,
And I am proud to be heard.
I work towards my pin,
And I will always wear a grin.

If it's hard I shall believe,
Because in my mind, I will always achieve.
I will also use my protective hand,
Because I sometimes misunderstand.

I will be independent,
Like my own secret agent.
I will discover my own sense of self,
And not just leave it on a shelf.

I will always have a choice,
And a chance to show my voice.
I am special, unique and kind,
And I will always have an open mind.

I can handle my emotions,
And in my work take promotions.

I will progress my learning journey,
An individual, that is me.

## Alex Waller (9)
Brooklands Farm Primary School, Milton Keynes

# If I Were In Charge Of The World

If I were in charge of the world,
I'd cancel humming,
Mornings, hunting and also yellow.

If I were in charge of the world,
There'd be unicorns,
Dinosaurs and chocolate ice cream with nuts.

If I were in charge of the world,
You wouldn't have bullying,
You wouldn't have rudeness,
You wouldn't have punching,
Or "Don't punch your brother!"
You wouldn't even have brothers.

If I were in charge of the world,
A chocolate ice cream would be a vegetable,
All fruit would be unhealthy.
And a person who sometimes forgets to talk,
And sometimes forgets to not talk
Would still be allowed to be in charge of the world.

**Emily Short (9)**
Brooklands Farm Primary School, Milton Keynes

# If I Were In Charge Of The World

If I were in charge of the world,
I'd cancel loud children, painful shots,
Donald Trump and also disgusting things.

If I were in charge of the world,
there'd be talking puppies,
flying unicorns,
and ice cream for breakfast.

If I were in charge of the world,
you wouldn't have Weetabix,
you wouldn't have Cheerios,
you wouldn't have mud or liquid glue,
you wouldn't even have mean people.

If I were in charge of the world,
ice cream would be a vegetable,
all chocolate would be fruit,
and a person who sometimes forgets to wash,
and sometimes forgets to shower,
would still be allowed to be in charge of the world!

**Emilie Higgs (8)**
Brooklands Farm Primary School, Milton Keynes

# Change Is Fine

I started in Year One
Where I began
Playing with my teddy bear
I became a little mare.

Then came Year Two
Everything seemed so new
Always hurting my arm
I became so calm.

Quickly came Year Three
Moving like a bee
Transferred to another site
I saw my primary light.

Year Four hit me
But I was still a little pea
Another day on my path
Until came my bath.

Year Five came alive
Scaring me terribly

Something stood in my way which wasn't expected
That's when I realised I was selected.

Here came Year Six
It was an emotional mix
Thinking of my reputation
I believe I hit my expectation.

## Em-Jaye Goddphin (10)
Brooklands Farm Primary School, Milton Keynes

# If I Were In Charge Of The World

If I were in charge of the world,
I'd cancel school, robbers, spiders
and also Donald Trump.

If I were in charge of the world,
there'd be all new phones, pets,
fluffy sofas, and flying people.

If I were in charge of the world,
you wouldn't have cars,
you wouldn't have toys,
you wouldn't have guns or brothers,
you wouldn't even have sisters!

If I were in charge of the world,
a chocolate ice cream and smores
would be vegetables.
All ice cream and marshmallows
would be vegetables
and a person who forgets to read,
and sometimes forgets to lead

would still be allowed
to be in charge of the world!

## Rehan Khokhar (9)
Brooklands Farm Primary School, Milton Keynes

# My Change

Year One, time for fun
First day, didn't want to leave Mum
Done for fun.

Here is Year Two
Our water is in a glass
Just like a class.

Here is Year Three, flying like a bee
Open the door, here is more
Rainforest leaves, please do the rest
To make the trees grow.

Year Four, I joined a new school
My friends were so cool.
Not being a fool
Having a laugh
Not distracted
But it is attractive.

Year Five, I was really fun
So I decided to hum
Ready to leave

So I can achieve
Just believe.

Year Six
Barely alive, hardly survived
Almost there, just one more year
No more tears.

## Amelia Mustafa (10)
Brooklands Farm Primary School, Milton Keynes

# If I Were In Charge Of The World

If I were in charge of the world,
I'd cancel slugs, coughs, colds
and also long books.

If I were in charge of the world,
there'd be flying cars, short tests
and short school days.

If I were in charge of the world,
you wouldn't have bullies,
you wouldn't have naughty sisters,
you wouldn't have carrots,
you wouldn't have to write
as there wouldn't be any pencils.

If I were in charge of the world,
a chocolate cake would be a vegetable,
all chocolate would be a vegetable
and a person who sometimes forgets to brush
and sometimes forgets to bathe
would still be allowed to be in charge of the world!

## Sarina Lawrence (8)
Brooklands Farm Primary School, Milton Keynes

# If I Were In Charge Of The World

If I were in charge of the world,
I'd cancel time, homework and illness.

If I were in charge of the world,
there'd be talking animals,
invisibility powers and Harry Potter wands.

If I were in charge of the world,
you wouldn't have behaviour charts,
you wouldn't have show-offs or bullies,
you wouldn't even have horrible people.

If I were in charge of the world,
a chocolate trifle would be a vegetable,
all boys would be the dumbest people in the world,
and a person who sometimes forgets
to get up in the morning,
and sometimes forgets to go to bed
would still be allowed to be in charge of the world.

**Kiera Whitham (8)**
Brooklands Farm Primary School, Milton Keynes

# If I Were In Charge Of The World

If I were in charge of the world,
I'd cancel peas, carrots, zoos
and also Donald Trump.

If I were in charge of the world,
there'd be gold, Gucci and diamonds.

If I were in charge of the world,
you wouldn't have work,
you wouldn't have school,
you wouldn't have sharks
or hear "Eat your peas!"
you wouldn't even have peas.

If I were in charge of the world,
chocolate would be a vegetable,
all cupcakes would be a vegetable
and a person who sometimes
forgets to brush their teeth
and sometimes forgets to flush the toilet
would still be allowed to be in charge of the world!

**Julie Ann Donbeinaa (9)**
Brooklands Farm Primary School, Milton Keynes

# If I Were In Charge Of The World

If I were in charge of the world,
I'd cancel Monday evenings, black teeth,
Fortnite and also war.

If I were in charge of the world,
there would be more money for everyone,
real superpowers and Nintendo Switches for free!

If I were in charge of the world,
you wouldn't have night lights,
you wouldn't have rules,
you wouldn't have bedtime or cabbage,
you wouldn't even have peas!

If I were in charge of the world,
a bag of popcorn would be a vegetable,
all 12-rated movies would be PGs,
and a person who forgets to wash their hands,
would still be allowed to be in charge of the world!

**Miami Maddison John (8)**
Brooklands Farm Primary School, Milton Keynes

# If I Were In Charge Of The World

If I were in charge of the world,
I'd cancel zoos,
Donald Trump,
Justin Beiber and also guns.

If I were in charge of the world,
There'd be jewellery,
Gold money and
Flying carpets all over.

If I were in charge of the world,
You wouldn't have pants,
You wouldn't have rags,
You wouldn't have wine
Or cigarettes,
You wouldn't even smoke.

If I were in charge of the world,
Marshmallows and crisps would be vegetables,
All milkshakes will be milk,
And a person who forgets to drink

And sometimes forgets to eat
Would still be allowed to be in charge of the world!

**Rupert Vibush Sripathy (8)**
Brooklands Farm Primary School, Milton Keynes

# Change

Once, I was in Year One
That was when I began
I never came to school without my bear
Then I would be able to bare.

Then came Year Two
When everything was new
I get smarter every day
But then begin to march.

Here is Year Three
I took my key
To open a door
To go and explore.

I was now in my new school
I made a new friend who is cool
What shall I do to now achieve?
Maybe open, grow and believe.

Here is Year Five
My wellbeing was also a five

I knew what to do
So I grew.

Now Year Six
It was a mix
Then I met my new teacher
I was ready to meet you!

## Priscilla Otchere (10)
Brooklands Farm Primary School, Milton Keynes

# If I Were In Charge Of The World

If I were in charge of the world,
I'd cancel presidents
and have hero movies,
sweets and also soda.

If I were in charge of the world,
there'd be no mental health,
no sadness,
and no bullies.

If I were in charge of the world,
you wouldn't have slime,
you wouldn't have school,
you wouldn't have KFC
and you wouldn't have Donald Trump.

If I were in charge of the world,
a cake would be a vegetable,
all 18-rated movies would be PG,
a person who forgets to brush their teeth

and forgets to brush their hair
would still be allowed to be in charge of the world!

## Lichelle Schumachers (9)
Brooklands Farm Primary School, Milton Keynes

# If I Were In Charge Of The World

If I were in charge of the world,
I'd cancel Donald Trump,
natural disasters, sickness
and also any other bad stuff.

If I were in charge of the world,
there'd be everlasting life
and anything you pray to Jehovah for,
he will give it to you.

If I were in charge of the world,
you wouldn't have plastic, prisons, hatred,
you wouldn't hear "You have cancer".

If I were in charge of the world,
any chocolate or candy
would become a vegetable,
all movies would be U-rated
and a person who forgets to eat
and forgets to drink
would still be allowed in charge of the world!

**Jeffrey Kacou (8)**
Brooklands Farm Primary School, Milton Keynes

# If I Were In Charge Of The World

If I were in charge of the world,
I'd cancel vegetables, boxing,
money and also kings.

If I were in charge of the world,
there'd be ice creams, free dogs
and Christmas every day.

If I were in charge of the world,
you wouldn't have presidents,
you wouldn't have shops,
you wouldn't have work,
you wouldn't need to drink
and you wouldn't have a bedtime.

If I were in charge of the world,
eggs, bacon, ice cream or fries
would be vegetables.
and a person who sometimes forgets to flush
or sometimes forgets to eat
would still be allowed to be in charge of the world!

**Jaime Gomez (8)**
Brooklands Farm Primary School, Milton Keynes

# If I Were In Charge Of The World

If I were in charge of the world,
I'd cancel boys, sharks,
lightning and also short hair.
If I were in charge of the world,
There'd be swimming all day,
Chocolates and sweets.

If I were in charge of the world,
You wouldn't have homework,
You wouldn't have school,
You wouldn't have black clothes,
Or hitting,
You wouldn't even have punched.

If I were in charge of the world,
A strawberry ice cream would be a vegetable,
All fish would be a fruit,
And a person who sometimes forgets to flush,
And sometimes forgets to brush,
Would still be allowed to be in charge of the world.

**Lina El-Majdki (9)**
Brooklands Farm Primary School, Milton Keynes

# If I Were In Charge Of The World

If I were in charge of the world,
I'd cancel homework, toilet passes,
Unicorns and also football.

If I were in charge of the world,
There'd be no worksheets, no cleaning and
*No* yellow!

If I were in charge of the world,
You wouldn't have poorly people,
You wouldn't have chores,
You wouldn't have flats,
You wouldn't even have books.

If I were in charge of the world,
A chocolate ice cream with a flake is a vegetable
and a person who sometimes forgets to shower
and sometimes forgets to get out of bed
would still be allowed to be in charge of the world.

**Mia Rose Stevens (9)**
Brooklands Farm Primary School, Milton Keynes

# My Changes

My journey had begun
Exploring all lands
But it all came to an end
As I began to move school.

Now I'm in Year Two
In a new school
Making new friends
Better than you.

Now I'm at Brooklands Farm as well as Year Three
Moving again
Really confused
How to survive.

Year Four came by
Quicker than a flash
Then I met a creature
He was really my teacher.

Year Five was now
Man I'm old
Mr Creature

Still my teacher
Sadly he left
Nice for him!

Finally Year Six
Ready to mix
SATs are soon
Do I need a spoon?

## Amberley Chikukwa (11)
Brooklands Farm Primary School, Milton Keynes

# Individual

Be the person you want to be,
An individual person for the world to see.
A place where our talents roam free,
And a better place for you and me.

Be you in your own way,
But don't listen to what others say.

Different as you are,
And be yourself no matter who you are.

Everyone may not agree,
Some like gold, some like green,
Or climb up the highest growing tree.
Beyond the hill I see,
Sometimes believing just like me.

From individual to achieve,
To let us all believe.
Even though it might not be easy
I'll be individual and everybody sees me.

**Aya Houria Mouhi (10)**
Brooklands Farm Primary School, Milton Keynes

# If I Were In Charge Of The World

If I were in charge of the world,
I'd cancel bad guys, carrots,
chicken and also pie.

If I were in charge of the world,
there'd be kind people
and everyone would be rich.

If I were in charge of the world,
you wouldn't have wild animals,
you wouldn't have volcanoes,
you wouldn't have smoking or guns and bows,
you wouldn't have weapons.

If I were in charge of the world,
bubblegum would be a vegetable,
all flowers would be big and strong
and a person who sometimes forgets to flush,
would still be allowed to be in charge of the world!

**Anna Kotyza (8)**
Brooklands Farm Primary School, Milton Keynes

# If I Were In Charge Of The World

If I were in charge of the world,
I'd cancel football, noisy people,
snot and also Fortnite.

If I were in charge of the world,
there's be unicorns, dogs, cats, and dragons.

If I were in charge of the world,
you wouldn't have a bedtime,
you wouldn't have pens,
you wouldn't have cars or rats
and you wouldn't be sad.

If I were in charge of the world,
a sweet would be a vegetable,
and a person who sometimes forgets to be happy
and sometimes forgets to be helpful
would still be allowed to be in charge.

### Ellie Patricia Keeble (9)
Brooklands Farm Primary School, Milton Keynes

# Individual

Be the person you want to be
An honest individual for the world to see
A place where our talents can roam free
A better world for you and me

Be yourself in your own way
Ignore what others may say
Independent as you are
Listen to yourself and you'll go far

Be the person you know you are
Always try to raise the bar
Try to be original
Listen to this and you'll never fail.

Never stop and you will achieve
By taking steps on your learning journey
Beyond the hills, I can see
Everyone supporting me.

**Anna Ungureanu (10)**
Brooklands Farm Primary School, Milton Keynes

# If I Were In Charge Of The World

If I were in charge of the world,
I'd cancel slugs, colds, coughs
and also long books.

If I were in charge of the world,
there'd be no SATs, mansions and flying cars.

If I were in charge of the world,
you wouldn't have parents,
you wouldn't have illnesses,
you wouldn't have bugs.

If I were in charge of the world,
yummy cake would be a vegetable
and a person who forgets
to have a bath and forgets to flush
would still be allowed to be
in charge of the world!

**Ridhima Das (8)**
Brooklands Farm Primary School, Milton Keynes

# Be The Change You Want To Be

Be the change I want to see,
A better individual I can be.
A place my learning can roam free,
Making me the best learner I can be.

Listen to my thoughts please,
Who knows what this verse achieves.
By opening my heart I can succeed,
It's possible, my brain believes.

Sometimes I may not see,
Some like maths, others like projects.
I will climb up the working wall,
Beyond the learning journey,
Learning is what they see.

**Ryan Coppin (10)**
Brooklands Farm Primary School, Milton Keynes

# I'm Going On Ten

It is a new year
Individualism is my new tier
This is my new year
I am happy for my new life.

It is a journey
This is my learning
I am turning
Into an individual.

This is my turning
I better get learning
I am burning
To do some more learning.

I'm going on ten
It's time to explore
It's time for more
Individualism.

It's time to strive
As I dive

Into the pool of Year Five
It's time to get alive.

## Nathaniel James Wood (9)
Brooklands Farm Primary School, Milton Keynes

# If I Were In Charge Of The World

If I were in charge of the world,
I'd cancel boys, lunch detention, math lessons,
and Donald Trump.

If I were in charge of the world,
there'd be no Fortnite,
lunch detention for boys
and boys would turn into girls.

If I were in charge of the world,
you wouldn't have football,
you wouldn't have singing,
you wouldn't have talking boys
or singing boys aged nine
and you wouldn't have any boys!

**Wiktoria Ostrowska (9)**
Brooklands Farm Primary School, Milton Keynes

# Year Five Now

I was in Year Four, entering Year Five
Now I get to change.
I'm going to change with my open heart
I'm polite, I'm helpful, I'm funny in sort of a way.
I am strong, not wrong
It's fun in Year Five
My project is Kings and Queens
In Year Five, I'm going to try and be kind
Even if it's the hard side
I know my work can roam free
Even if it's hard
New year, new people,
New friends to be!

## Mina Fatima (9)
Brooklands Farm Primary School, Milton Keynes

# Growing Up

**C** hanging age is exciting because you get presents,
**H** aving more fun at school because you have more things to do,
**A** new set of maths and harder homework too,
**N** ext, you will get even harder maths because you do real-life maths
**G** rowing up is very tough because you need to do harder stuff like earn more money
**E** very day I get a headache because I listen to so much stuff and have to do amazing maths and projects.

## Stephen Lam (8)
Brooklands Farm Primary School, Milton Keynes

# Change

Be the change you want to see
A harder journey for you and me
An individual is our next turn
A whole new road for me to learn.

Independent learners we will be
Hard-working, kind and funny
A new school year we are awaiting
Eager to start celebrating.

I climb out of the pod of Year Four
Expecting a change before
Diving into the pod of Year Five
We might just be able to make it out alive.

**Olivia Sparrow (9)**
Brooklands Farm Primary School, Milton Keynes

# All About My Changes

**C** hanges happened all the time when I was little,
**H** appily, I moved two houses in my life
**A** t the colossal shops, I had to sit in the hard trolley
**N** ever at the funfair, I didn't go on big rides
**G** etting in the car was because I got to put a pebble in the jar
**E** aster is fun for kids but, when you get older, it starts to get boring and a waste of your time because you just have to work!

## Liam Arslan (7)
Brooklands Farm Primary School, Milton Keynes

# Individual

Everybody back at school ready to learn,
Individuals are ready to turn.
Taking ownership is what we do.

When we come for you.
Being respectful is the most delightful way,
But being full of energy has to stay.
Being motivated is the way to open your mind,
But sometimes you have to be a little kind.
Being supportive makes a good friend,
Motivation and kindness we have to send.

**Tyson Romeo John (10)**
Brooklands Farm Primary School, Milton Keynes

# Weather

**C** louds drifting, slowly in the warm, ocean breeze.
**H** urricanes destroying cities, schools, homes, and caves.
**A** nnoying weather for the playful cute children who want to run.
**N** ew children want to play but the roaring, rubbish rain stops them.
**G** reat earthquakes happen and make huge holes.
**E** arthquakes opening, cracking, shaking the hard concrete ground.

## Leah Quigley (7)
Brooklands Farm Primary School, Milton Keynes

# Changing Age

- **C** hanging age is hard because you need to do harder maths
- **H** ard maths is actually boring because it is easy
- **A** t your birthday, it is fun because you get presents
- **N** ext year, you will get harder maths, but you will get more presents as well
- **G** row your maths so you can be a famous mathematician
- **E** very day do two hours of math to be a famous mathematician.

**Maher Parikh (8)**
Brooklands Farm Primary School, Milton Keynes

# Weather

- **C** louds slowly drifting in the warm ocean breeze, destroying homes and cities,
- **H** urricanes destroying homes and cities,
- **A** nnoying weather for the kids that are playing and having fun,
- **N** oisy hurricanes swishing around the air,
- **G** ood weather when people are at the beach,
- **E** arthquakes opening, cracking, shaking of the ground.

**Marley Steven Maison (7)**
Brooklands Farm Primary School, Milton Keynes

# Change Through The School

**C** ancel all the bad memories through the school
**H** ang on to things you need to keep cool
**A** rrange them year after year after year to remember
**N** ever give up when changing your life
**G** ather all the things you've done and store them
**E** very day the school will change with happiness.

**Millie Marjorie Germain (7)**
Brooklands Farm Primary School, Milton Keynes

# Changes

**C** hanges are fun
**H** aving a change is just doing something different
**A** change doesn't have to be something you don't like
**N** othing gets done if you don't change
**G** uess what? I had to move house, it was scary
**E** veryone is lovely when you change.

## Toni Akinsanya (7)
Brooklands Farm Primary School, Milton Keynes

# Change

**C** hanging friends can be a difficult time,
**H** aving different friends in a different school can be scary.
**A** re you having fun in your new school?
**N** ew teachers can also be scary.
**G** et a great future in your new school,
**E** very friendship can be difficult.

## Pahal Patel (7)
Brooklands Farm Primary School, Milton Keynes

# Weather

C louds moving, drifting in the ocean breeze
H urricanes destroying homes and cities
A nnoying weather for children who want to play
N oisy doors shutting
G ood weather and sunshine in the air
E arthquake opening, cracking, shaking the hard ground.

## Daisey Adams (8)
Brooklands Farm Primary School, Milton Keynes

# Weather

**C** louds slowly drifting into the warm sky
**H** urricanes destroy sites
**A** nnoying weather for children when they want to play
**N** oisy weather closes doors
**G** iant earthquakes hit somewhere
**E** arthquakes open cracks, shaking the hard ground.

## Kieran Peter Allwood (8)
Brooklands Farm Primary School, Milton Keynes

# Changes In My Life

**C** ountries go to change
**H** oly festivals change and I learn from different countries
**A** house I used to live in changed
**N** ot worried about anything if things are changing
**G** oing to different places
**E** njoying new changes in my life.

## Sanah Kumar (7)
Brooklands Farm Primary School, Milton Keynes

# Weather

**C** louds in the blue-white sky
**H** ow would you move a cloud?
**A** valanches can hurt lots of people
**N** atural disasters are very dangerous and scary
**G** iant earthquakes hit countries far away
**E** arthquakes can be extremely scary.

## Riley Childs (8)
Brooklands Farm Primary School, Milton Keynes

# Weather

**C** louds coming up in the wide sky
**H** ot, bright, yellow sun
**A** nnoying sun for kids that want to play!
**N** ew people are playing in the sun
**G** lobal warming around polar bears is not good
**E** arthquakes shake the ground

**Mugdha Gowri Basanth (7)**
Brooklands Farm Primary School, Milton Keynes

# Change

**C** hanging to a new season is great fun
**H** as three months in each one
**A** season is winter, summer, spring, and autumn
**N** ever in the middle
**G** rowing leaves on trees and falling off
**E** nds after three-four months.

## Layla Sharman (7)
Brooklands Farm Primary School, Milton Keynes

# Singapore

**C** hanging countries took a while
**H** ow it brought me a little smile
**A** nd I loved Singapore
**N** ow go see for yourself so you can say what you saw
**G** o run free into wild parks
**E** nd boring jobs and parts.

## Ella Sparrow (7)
Brooklands Farm Primary School, Milton Keynes

# Change Eating

**C** an you try new foods?
**H** ave you tried mustard?
**A** change in eating food is fun
**N** ew food is beautiful
**G** reat mustard is brilliant and incredible
**E** ven though it smells disgusting, it tastes good.

## Ewan George Roberts (8)
Brooklands Farm Primary School, Milton Keynes

# Natural Disaster

**C** old, icy, falling snow from an avalanche.
**H** ot lava from an eruption of a volcano.
**A** unty drowned from a flood.
**N** atural disasters!
**G** osh, it's a whirlpool on land!
**E** arth has volcanoes!

## Pranav Gupta (7)
Brooklands Farm Primary School, Milton Keynes

# Well Being

**C** hange your facial expression
**H** ave an excellent 'gotcha' smile
**A** high wellbeing with lots of confidence
**N** o angry moments
**G** ood behaviour around the school
**E** normous achievements!

## Kailen Helm (8)
Brooklands Farm Primary School, Milton Keynes

# Change

**C** hanging my sister's school,
**H** as meant I don't see her anymore,
**A** new school for my sister is great for her,
**N** ew school means a lot,
**G** rowing a new school,
**E** xcellent work Lacie.

**Lillie-Mae Weller (7)**
Brooklands Farm Primary School, Milton Keynes

# Change

**C** hange schools and make a new learning journey
**H** ave a different lifestyle
**A** mazing house to live in
**N** ever go with a stranger
**G** row your learning and make it better
**E** ver changing clothes.

## Aimee Joy Haggis (7)
Brooklands Farm Primary School, Milton Keynes

# Change

**C** hanging my language
**H** as helped me to grow
**A** nd helped me find more people I know
**N** o one knows how scary it can be
**G** oing to a new school and being me
**E** veryone can learn something new.

## Taimaa Al Haj Ali (7)
Brooklands Farm Primary School, Milton Keynes

# Games

**C** heck if the games are good
**H** ow to play a hard game?
**A** n early game that you can play
**N** o one played that game
**G** ames are good but hard ones aren't
**E** njoy playing games!

## Borys Sawicki (7)
Brooklands Farm Primary School, Milton Keynes

# Changes

**C** hanging year groups to Year Three
**H** ad made me feel different
**A** nd we have rules and
**N** ew behaviour
**G** oing to Year Three feels really different
**E** ven we have a new teacher.

## Anya Reddy (7)
Brooklands Farm Primary School, Milton Keynes

# Change

**C** hanging schools and houses
**H** ave I decided which school will I go to?
**A** new set of rules
**N** ew friends
**G** rowing in different years
**E** ven a learning zone four or five!

## Kiara Patel (7)
Brooklands Farm Primary School, Milton Keynes

# Wellbeing

**C** hange your good expression
**H** ave an excellent 'gotcha' smile
**A** high wellbeing
**N** o anger
**G** ood pace to finish work and be proud
**E** normous achievements!

## Calum O'Sullivan (8)
Brooklands Farm Primary School, Milton Keynes

# Changing Year Group

**C** hanging class year by year,
**H** as me wondering where I'll appear,
**A** new book day by day,
**N** ew rules for expectations,
**G** oing into lessons,
**E** ven learning.

**Jayden Lau (7)**
Brooklands Farm Primary School, Milton Keynes

# Change Growing Up

**C** hanging my age
**H** aving a Year Three classroom
**A** big girl now
**N** ew exciting hard things to do
**G** iving people answers to do
**E** veryone gets to do something new.

## Leah Mae Wears (7)
Brooklands Farm Primary School, Milton Keynes

# Changing My Life

**C** hanging is different
**H** aving a sister
**A** rranging things
**N** ew swimming lessons
**G** etting my new house ready
**E** ating new things.

## Karishma Patel (7)
Brooklands Farm Primary School, Milton Keynes

# The Bear-Boar And Me!

Where am I? I can't see,
Maybe in a world of fantasy.
I looked left, I looked right,
A massive bang gave me a terrible fright.
Something moved, I swear it did,
So off I ran somewhere and hid.
Then suddenly, a blinding flash!
But before I had a chance to dash,
In front of me, I saw,
What looked like a bear mixed with a boar?
"Oh my golly, sweet lemon pies!"
I could not believe my eyes.
But don't worry reader, it was fine in the end.
Me and the bear-boar became best friends!

**Rivkah Richards-Gray (9)**
Haddenham Community Junior School, Haddenham

# Game Play

What's up y'all? Let's start with a game,
Before we do that, let me tell you my name.
My name is Salah-Udeen Nabi,
We're about to play and I'm so happy.
Let's go guys,
Wait that's just a lie.
Let's go now,
I wonder how.
It's only going to work when you drink this jug
*Chug! Chug! Chug!*
We're going in through the portal of doom.
Hold your ears there'll be a loud *boom!*
We're in the game,
The game's called irreversible that's so lame.
Got a pickaxe,
Let's level up to the max.
Why's he standing in the open.
I just killed you. CooCoo782.
Oh no, 1v1
I'm done, I'm done
Wait, I killed him, that was fun!

**Salah-Udeen Nabi (9)**
Millbrook Combined School, High Wycombe

# Wonderland Dream

I once got dragged into a flag,
And landed on a marshmallow,
I jumped up and down but landed on the ground,
And saw a giant watermelon,
I looked inside and saw a bat with a very small hat,
And it said, "Hey."
I looked once back,
But then a magic key turned up,
He said to me, "Follow me."
And once again he pushed me,
I teleported through the goo,
And once got stuck on the loo,
I got flushed into the drain,
And met my mum in a pain,
But then a cheetah came and took her away,
When she was gone, I met a big troll,
He gobbled me up and went for a stroll,
I saw a hat with a very fluffy cat,
And once again, I got pulled in the hat,
Then fell off the troll.

Then I saw a three-headed dog,
I walked away but the dog said, "Hey."
I met Harry Potter,
He got his wand and cast a spell,
It sent me back home,
My face was a groan,
It was a dream,
I opened my eyes,
Then fell back to sleep.

## Mimi Burrough (10)
Millbrook Combined School, High Wycombe

# My Crazy World

Life is weirdly nice around here,
Although some say I live a pretty crazy life,
And I know exactly why.
During the night, my world is turned
Into a place of darkness.

The night is when the aliens are roaming about.
Patrolling each and every area
To see if anyone comes out.
I don't dare step out of my home,
And if anyone does we receive a strict warning.
When we've used them all up,
There is no turning back to happiness.

Back to Wonderland,
It's as wild as can be,
Flying horses,
Bunnies hopping on clouds.
I get my bucket to collect some chocolate
From the river and chug it all down.

It's night in Wonderland,
And I'm safely tucked up in my bed.

I'm thinking about what the next day will bring,
A normal day or an everyday crazy day?

## Ramisa Hussain (10)
Millbrook Combined School, High Wycombe

# The Savage Robot Arms

One beautiful, happy day,
Where the people stay.
A plane was accidentally delayed,
And it was *not* okay!
The robots have escaped,
But with a trace.
They were taken down,
Without a sound.
They didn't know that there was a catch.
Their arms were alive, there's over fifty-five!
There was no plan to stop the robots.
They were kidnapped,
And pushed over.
There was chaos everywhere!
Now everything has become bad,
We had to stop it before it was red.
Suddenly, I found a switch,
To deconstruct things.
I set it to the robot,
And saw the result.

Everything was good!
We were happy,
But something disappeared.,
And it was nasty.
No one was around,
So I ran hastily.

## Jason Frimpong (9)
Millbrook Combined School, High Wycombe

# Pandas Acting Like Monkeys

Pandas acting like monkeys, how strange!
Why do they think they have to change?
Not eating their bamboo
Just going ooh, ooh, ooh
What more could change?
They started tickling their armpits
Ew, how gross,
At least they're not leaving bananas on the carpets
I hope they don't get to close.

They went on an adventure
Where are they going to go?
And why on earth are they wearing bows?
They ended up on the beach
And tried to reach
For the shiny green sea.

At the end of the day
They made their way back home
PJs on, hair brushed, ate bamboo chips

Put on their clips
And swing into bed
Pillows under their head
And pretended to be dead!

**Sophie Weston (9)**
Millbrook Combined School, High Wycombe

# Exploding The Moon

I am so mad!
I am also a dad!
I am flying in a rocket with everything I need,
As I am planning my evil deed.
I had a dream when I was a kid,
But I altered that just a bit.
The dream I had altered is just as good,
But has a bit more action.
And certainly will make a big reaction.
My rocket's made of cheese,
And I always like to read.
But then *boom!*
The people on Earth are meeting their doom!
The mooney moon,
Has gone *boom!*
But hey, what's this?
The weeks are getting hotter!
I feel like melted butter!
I read and read and read, but no night came,
I thought the weather would be the same!

**Senthur Senthilnathan (10)**
Millbrook Combined School, High Wycombe

# The New Girl On The Haunted Farm

New girl, new farm, a new place to explore
One animal, two more, too many to count
Falling from the sky, wait they are on rainbows
What animals fall from the sky?

Rabbit, tiger, horse and more every animal
Including a bull.
Voices no one there
Animals talking in human voices.
Creeping you out or not
You won't guess what's next.

Flying saucers, one, two, three, counting them up,
Animals as aliens, aliens as animals.
Creeping me out I don't like it
I quit from this haunted farm

Do not enter ever again!

**Millie Zena Pearce (9)**
Millbrook Combined School, High Wycombe

# It's Here The Dragon!

Oh no! Oh no!
Is that it
I can't! I can't
Not a chance
It beams so hotly like a ratatat
You have to run away
Away, away!
It's near, it's near.

It's here! It's here!
It shines like stars
It's hot and red as the planet Mars
The time goes *tick tock, tick tock*
You can't stop it.

Oh no! Oh no!
It's gobbling me up
I won't survive
Just help! Just help!
That one time come on, come on.
He's got my feet
Just help, just help, right now!

I'm done! I'm done!
Forever and ever he's eating me right now.

## Emilia Czech (11)
Millbrook Combined School, High Wycombe

# Funny

Why is Big Shaq there?
Why has Hashim got so much hair?
Why does Olus always talk about an ugly bear?

Why did Olus sit on a nail?
Why did Dyan turn quite pale?
Why did Hashim swallow a snail?
No wonder why he felt quite frail.

Then I play Crew 2,
And I drink Mountain Dew,
I play Spider-Man,
He's friends with Jackie Chan.

Then I saw a clown,
With a gold crown,
He plays basketball,
He got won over by a cannonball.

There was a kid who wanted to go to Mars,
He met an alien who ate Mars bars.

**Aryan (10)**
Millbrook Combined School, High Wycombe

# In The Wonderland

Off I go into the wonderland,
Where I am eating rainbow crisps,
Look, look the dragon is curling my hair,
Oh no, what is this?
He has just painted my face!

In the sky, I can see
The colourful bees,
The grass is shining bright,
It gives the dragons a fright,
All the animals live in harmony!

The water is crystal clear,
There are exotic noises I can hear,
The apples on trees are red,
And one has just fallen on my head!
The sun is going down,
What a shame the day has ended,
But I'll come back tomorrow!

**Stefania Valentina Pantazi (10)**
Millbrook Combined School, High Wycombe

# Sweets 'n' Treats

Can you imagine a candy land,
For you and for me, it'll be totally fab,
Lollipop over here and there we have sweets,
For all of you peeps to share!

Gingerbread house for us to eat,
Gummy townhall is where we will meet,
You can even eat the sour heather,
And don't forget the gooey weather!

Sitting in the shop, it's your last hour,
People coming from the door as tall as a tower,
People trading for money, it's mad,
As I look closer, a figure emerges,
Wait that's me,
I'm very bad!

**Hassan Bin Suleman Hussain (10)**
Millbrook Combined School, High Wycombe

# Just A Silly Old Dream

The River Wye in the sky,
Riding a unicorn down the rainbow,
A faraway galaxy way up high,
Oh wow, just a silly old dream.

Seeing the sky way down low,
That's a really nice scene,
Santa always just says ho,
Oh wow, just a silly old dream.

The river Wye in the sky,
Riding a unicorn down the rainbow,
A faraway galaxy way up high,
Oh wow, just a silly old dream.

Dreams mess with your head,
You always get confused,
Don't forget to sharpen your lead,
Oh wow, just a silly dream.

**Mia Lashbrook (10)**
Millbrook Combined School, High Wycombe

# Driving A Plane On The Street

Driving a plane on the street,
While people make their houses neat.

Stuck in a queue,
While people's kites flew.

The plane is green,
So everybody thinks it's clean.

My plane is loud,
But quiet in the clouds.

My passengers are cool,
Because they swim in their plane's pool.

I can't hear a thing,
While people's tiny phones ring.

Because I'm driving a plane on the road,
While I see a toad!

**Faiqa Khan (9)**
Millbrook Combined School, High Wycombe

# Flying Books

I was sat in the library,
Choosing a book.
I started to sneeze,
The book started to fly around me.
I picked one up and started to read.

I stopped sneezing,
I took one home and,
Carried on reading.
I took it on holiday,
To America to Donald Trump's house.
The book had a meeting with Donald Trump.

It went to stop the violence,
And stop people getting murdered.

Then the flying book went
Back to the library.

**Umair Hussain (10)**
Millbrook Combined School, High Wycombe

# Beware Of The Shark

One day, I will lick a shark,
When it's very dark,
I'll sneak out of the house,
Very quietly, just like a mouse.
Down Rouse Road, there is a beach,
I had done enough
Swimming lessons with Mr Bleach.

The next morning, I was walking in the sea,
Suddenly, I saw something swimming behind me.
It waved and smiled with its raw teeth,
I walked back to the beach.
I thought I was going to scream,
But then we shared some ice cream!

**Maryam Fakraz (9)**
Millbrook Combined School, High Wycombe

# The Magic Tree

I wonder what's inside?
I stand in front of the door,
I look down on the floor,
And all that I could see,
Is just a cup of tea,
When I'm inside,
I've got nowhere to hide,
Here comes the owner,
And he looks at the toaster,
The toaster exploded.
"I did that," the owner said.
"My friend is in there!"
"Hey, you! Come back here!"
All that I can say
Is just, "Run away!"

**Michal Zablocki (9)**
Millbrook Combined School, High Wycombe

# Walking Through The Air

Walking through the air is such a breeze,
I'm so glad that I won't freeze!
Up and up and up I go,
Soon I will float around.
Out of the atmosphere into space!
There is no way back to my home base.
I want to get to my base.
It's okay I am now living in space.
I am living on the moon now and it is great.
Instead of the cheese on Earth,
The moon is made out of cheese.
It is so delicious.

## Tanvi Ramkissoom (9)
Millbrook Combined School, High Wycombe

# Thunder Land

Once I went to Thunder Land,
It was very wicked and cool
Once I went to Thunder Land,
I saw a great big pool
Once I went to Thunder Land,
I saw the black stretchy hall
Once I went to Thunder Land,
I played with a ball
But then I stepped into a lightning hole
And said, "Eww that's disgusting!
The top's all dry but the bottom's all wet!
Oh why, oh why is there no net?"

**Jamilia Korb (9)**
Millbrook Combined School, High Wycombe

# Chicken Apocalypse

I fell off my bed onto the floor
Someone was knocking on my door
I went to see
Got punched in the knee
By a chicken
It's eight in the morning, why's dinner cooking?
I went to the park to have some fun
All I saw was chickens run
Where is everyone hiding
Something must have gone wrong
Chickens ate my brain
Blood flowed through my veins
I was alive
But how did I survive?

**Spencer Humphreys (10)**
Millbrook Combined School, High Wycombe

# The Ninja Watermelon

I once met a watermelon,
Who was also a ninja.
He was red, he was green,
But had not a spot of ginger!

He had angered the police,
And was escaping the city.
He leapt from roof to roof,
He scared a sleeping kitty.

The ninja fruit climbed,
Higher and higher,
Then it zipped down a very long wire.

He grabbed a bar and then he swung,
His round body, he now flung.

**George Risness (9)**
Millbrook Combined School, High Wycombe

# The Wild Pets

I washed my hands clearly
I got my leg right underneath the waterfall
Ohh, something caught my leg
It looked like a plant that was stuck to the ground
It was spiky, creamy, slimy and smelly
Why did I come here with a farting pickle
Burping cow and flying horse?
The animals snored a lot
The next day, we went exploring the forest
It was fun
For lunch, we had a curry with a bun.

## Nithuja Jegan (9)
Millbrook Combined School, High Wycombe

# The Big Elephant

I saw a big elephant at the zoo,
The trunk was so dirty but what could I do?
I decided to climb up the elephant
And splash water,
The elephant got out of control
And took me for a super ride,
He jumped over the massive fence,
I slipped off and fell into the sticky dirty mud,
I shook with anger and screamed,
I quickly got out of the mud,
And stomped all the way back home.

**Zaeem Ghauri (9)**
Millbrook Combined School, High Wycombe

# Halloween

We go along the darkened street,
This spooky Halloween,
Freddy dressed as a mummy,
Bandaged from head to feet,
Darren is dressed as Frankenstein,
His face sickly green,
Sarah dressed like a frightening ghost,
Wrapped up in a sheet,
I am dressed as Dracula,
My cape is red like blood and dark as night,
But I wish I knew who the zombie was,
Creeping along at the back.

**Bazagh (10)**
Millbrook Combined School, High Wycombe

# Unicorn World

Get a unicorn, not to worry,
It has only one horn.
It isn't as pointy as a thorn.
Go high up, eat a super-duper cloud.
Do what you want, sit at the front, scream so loud!
Ask them to do magic.
It can't be tragic.
It will be funny.
Bring what you want a cat, dog or even a bunny.
Don't worry, you won't get caught.
Come on tell me what have you thought?

**Barakaath Bashir (9)**
Millbrook Combined School, High Wycombe

# My Walnut

My precious walnut,
It beats the chestnut,
And the hazelnut,
And the coconut.
It beats every nut,
But its a tough nut.
Everyone uses a shortcut,
Away from my walnut.
It can cut,
In its hut.
Even though it's a tiny nut hut.
Its door automatically opens and shuts.
One day, along came Peanut,
He said, "What are you doing my friend Walnut?"

**Alexandra Dorina Sutic (10)**
Millbrook Combined School, High Wycombe

# Underwater Zoo

There's something in the water,
Oh no, it's my daughter.
Hopefully, she doesn't drown
While she's wearing my crown.
So I go into save her,
With my coat made of fur.
Then I see a zoo in the water with hippos dancing,
Then I was planting.
So I see a shark and freeze,
Then I run to the park.
I am now in the park with the shark,
*Arghh!*

**Amelia Hussain (9)**
Millbrook Combined School, High Wycombe

# The Day The Pandicorn Became My Pet

A pandicorn is a great guy,
I love him so much and that is why,
I made him my pet,
But I need to get,
Some food for him to eat.
What do they eat? I don't know?
Maybe they said it on the radio,
I ran to the shop and got some food,
But he said no, which was very rude,
I got rid of him and that is why,
A pandicorn is actually a horrible guy!

**Isabelle Alexander (9)**
Millbrook Combined School, High Wycombe

# The Crazy Birthday

I saw leaves dropping into my pocket
When I looked up, I saw a rocket
Then I ate a chip
I hurt my lip
After, I saw a buffalo dancing in the streets
I went to town to eat some treats
When I went out
I started to shout
"Look at that kite!"
Someone was crazy
And very very lazy
It was my birthday
And it was on a Thursday.

**Saif Ayub (9)**
Millbrook Combined School, High Wycombe

# The Magical World Of Animals

The dragon breathing fire,
The unicorns in the sky,
Flying like a hero,
Above the rate of zero,
Beneath the magical world's wall,
Lay the animals once and for all.

Learn to speak the animal language,
How do you do that?
I don't know how to,
Is it going to be bad?
What if I tell my parents,
They're going to be mad!

**Aleesha Saba (10)**
Millbrook Combined School, High Wycombe

# Walking On A Cloud

Walking on a cloud,
The sun goes down,
The sky gets dark,
I fall down.
*Argh!* My back hurts,
The cloud falls down and,
Throws me up in the sky.
The sun comes up and,
Everything gets bright and shiny.
Walking on a cloud,
I feel the fluffy cloud,
I hear the birds' sound,
I look down,
I see a different town.

## Manahil Javed (10)
Millbrook Combined School, High Wycombe

# Windsurfing Dog

A brave dog went windsurfing one day
His face was wet and covered in spray
The wind was blowing and blowing him along
The dog said, "You need to be really strong!"
He looked down and saw lots of fish
And started to think of cooking a dish
He wiped sweat from his brow using his left hand
A gust of wind pushed him back to dry land.

**Harvey Richards (9)**
Millbrook Combined School, High Wycombe

# Lessons In The Sky

I have lessons in the sky,
There are desks and chairs floating in the air.
Teachers standing on the clouds,
The sky is sunny, bright and shiny.
Children having fun,
Everyone screaming in the sky.
Kids reading books,
Teachers working with children.
All desks, chairs, everything
Is back on the ground again.
"Phew!"

**Ameera Amer (9)**
Millbrook Combined School, High Wycombe

# A Normal Day For Pigoatman

The day of the Pigoatman,
He ran smiling up and down,
Stealing magic all around,
He flicked and swooshed,
Sending people to Pandacorn,
A place for pandas and unicorns,
They gobbled and flushed the sweets around,
Got so fat the people exploded with a loud sound!

The Pigoatman dashed off,
With a terrible cough.

## Debby Adeorike Lawal (10)
Millbrook Combined School, High Wycombe

# Hampires!

**H** elp, we're scared of humans,
**A** m I a human? *Nope!*
**M** aybe next year,
**P** ut vampire and human together and you get hampire!
**I** don't like humans!
**R** eally rude humans!
**E** ek! Humans and vampires are now *hampires!*

Argh! I don't want to be a hampire!

## Indumini Wijerathne (9)
Millbrook Combined School, High Wycombe

# The Gingerbread House

In the middle of nowhere, without a sight,
I saw a gingerbread house in the night.
When I saw it, I went inside,
I saw delicious treats and I was filled with pride.
I ate some gingerbread, more than I should,
I was very full like a piece of wood.
In a while, I looked around,
I went upstairs and nothing made a sound.

**Thalia Sehmbi (9)**
Millbrook Combined School, High Wycombe

# Flying Fruits

Fruits flying in the air
And when I saw them, I didn't care
All fruits looked delicious
I tried licking the dishes
I ate an apple
And I felt like a bubble
I saw some fruits without a sight
I found them flying in the night
When I saw them they flew in my face
And I started moving all over the place.

## Sandra Mihaela Stoica (9)
Millbrook Combined School, High Wycombe

# The Crazy Monster Maths Book Under My Bed

A crazy monster maths book under my bed,
Argh! What shall I do?
Rip out its pages?
Cut off its head?

It runs around my bedroom,
Doing what it wants,
It scares me with big numbers,
So I killed it...
Now it's dead.

Hip, hip, hooray, now it's dead,
Now I can go back to bed.

**Zara Masood (10)**
Millbrook Combined School, High Wycombe

# Surfing On A Door

Surfing on a door is so much fun,
You can enjoy yourself in the sun,
I'll make sure I'll be there,
And also wet my hair.
I love surfing on a door,
You can learn so much more,
I saw something over there,
Oh, just a girl with black hair,
Are you going to surf?
Where, when and how?

**Nana-Yaa Sarpong (9)**
Millbrook Combined School, High Wycombe

# The Flying Cheesy Pickles

The flying cheesy pickles flew
I went to them and said "Ew!"
I said bye
Someone called out, "Die!"
I saw a plane underwater
And then I saw its daughter
The cheesy pickle grew wings
And he went to see the cheesy pickle king
I threw a tool
And it landed in the pool.

**Harrison Blackwell (10)**
Millbrook Combined School, High Wycombe

# Bubble Gum Lava

One sunny day, I woke up
I had a weird but crazy idea
About going surfing
On the volcano.
When I was surfing,
The hot, steep
And mountainous volcano
Was erupting
Out of nowhere came
Out bubblegum lava.
A blink of an eye
The lava chased me
Like a hideous
Man!

### Hafsah Zaman (9)
Millbrook Combined School, High Wycombe

# Dragon Danger

I'm in my Wonderland
Having fun and eating candy.
Suddenly, fear!
I see a candy dragon.
Run!
One bite, ouch,
Two bites, ouch,
Three bites, ouch.
And now he's done.
I'm having fabulous fun.
But the bad thing is,
I've got dragon marks all over my skin!

**Adam Kharbouch (9)**
Millbrook Combined School, High Wycombe

# Flying Goat

In my boat,
I had hidden a flying goat,
But all of a sudden,
The goat flew to a city nearby,
Stealing flowers from a garden.
The goat was pink,
And his ears were black as ink.
I managed to catch him,
But he kicked me up and down,
Into the sky and back on the ground.

**Oskar Poprawa (9)**
Millbrook Combined School, High Wycombe

# Chocolate House

Everyone likes chocolate
Except for some people
There's different
Kinds of chocolate bars
Milk chocolate
Dark chocolate
White chocolate
And normal chocolate
Now, do you like chocolate?
There's a chocolate
House down
The road
You know!

**Hannan Hussain (9)**
Millbrook Combined School, High Wycombe

# Mot - Dog Danger

I polished the dog's fake teeth,
I got my arm right underneath,
He took the motorbike out,
But I had to shout,
My feet were bumpy,
But the dog's feet were lumpy,
So he was very grumpy,
The rocking chair was very rough,
But I was very tough.

**Namra Mahmood (9)**
Millbrook Combined School, High Wycombe

# The Picnic

I once saw a creature,
On the distant planet Mars,
It was just a few days ago,
When he gave me a bar,
He then laid out the mat,
And handed out the food,
Partied with his friends,
And gave us magic soup!

**Hashim Asim (10)**
Millbrook Combined School, High Wycombe

# The Destruction Of Earth

Volcanoes erupting
Earth quaking
Fire-breathing dragon
Children not knowing what is coming
Adults screaming
Children crying
*Boom!*
Earth is *destroyed!*

**Mohammed Ali Mehmood**
Millbrook Combined School, High Wycombe

# Smurf

I'm on Earth
With a blue smurf,
I love Nerf
And I love dabs,
I go to a lab,
I go to a gym
And get abs!

## Dylan Olando Derby (9)
Millbrook Combined School, High Wycombe

# Key
*A haiku*

The key to my heart
Is very hard to get to
It sits in my soul.

## Archie Julian Jeffries (11)
Millbrook Combined School, High Wycombe

# Poetry Wonderland

I fell down the rabbit hole,
And saw letters swirling around.
My eyes widened as I gasped in awe,
Before hitting a splintering ground.
The floor was made of pencil sharpenings,
I saw a river flowing with ink.
Beside me were paper boys and girls,
All working in perfect sync.
The sun was made from yellow rubber,
Houses made out of pen nibs.
Further away, grew lead trees,
Bearing juicy figs.
I had seen a new world;
A beautiful sight.
I had watched the people,
And their way of life.
I dusted myself off,
Standing upright.
It was time to go,
But the rabbit hole wasn't in sight.
I was stuck in Poetry Wonderland!

## Anushree Nikhil Kaluskar (10)
Woodside Junior School, Amersham

# Matt The Cat

I peered down the hole but it was dark and gloomy.
So I moved down a bit to where it was roomy
and slipped down and went round
until I landed flat on the ground.
When I looked up, I saw a big fat cat.
Right next to him was a little white cat,
they thought it was funny
and they laughed out loud.
They sat on a mat and jiggled around.
All of a sudden, a big rabbit appeared
and a little purple man with a long, white beard,
"Oh goody!" they shouted. "Let's have a party!
Somewhere we've hidden a great big Smartie!"

**Mattis Cook (8)**
Woodside Junior School, Amersham

# School Invaders

*Ssssshh!*
Listen
Can you hear them?
The school invaders are coming
Coming to feast on fun
Have you heard the legend?
No?
Well, listen,
The people of Amersham say…
For every school, they lay their eyes upon
The fun begins to grow
Candyfloss trees and lollipop apples
Chocolate fountains everywhere you go
Shoelaces are liquorice and gummy bears everywhere
Come on! Come on!
Let's go! Let's go!
Let's go to school
Follow me.

## Rosie Horton (10)
Woodside Junior School, Amersham

# The Mysterious Land

I fell off the cliff and swam in the sea,
That's when a dragon swallowed me up,
What a horrible thing to see.
He burped me out into a mystical land.
It was super, super weird,
I couldn't understand.
Monsters are not real.
Food cannot fly.
An orange is not a planet.
I don't know how to get by.
But there was an old story
Of how I could get home,
Make a wish, click my shoes,
*Whoosh*, off I go.

**Isabel Hibberd (10)**
Woodside Junior School, Amersham

# Playing Hopscotch With A Giant Dog

I was playing hopscotch on my own
Then a giant came over
He asked me to play with him
I said yes
We started to play again
No one won!

We play again
Still, no one won
Who would win?
The giant won
The giant went over the moon

The giant went home
The next day, he brought a dog
A very cute dog
We played with the dog

Last round
The dog won
That was the end of the giant!

**Kimberley Revel (9)**
Woodside Junior School, Amersham

# My Little Grindylow

My little grindylow,
Sweet as can be.
My little grindylow,
It loves me.

My little grindylow,
It's all mine.
My little grindylow,
An underwater shine.

My little grindylow,
Is a great companion.
My little grindylow,
Shows lots of passion.

My little grindylow,
You may be slimy.
My little grindylow,
You may be grimy,
But you are my little grindylow!

**Ajooni Jassy (10)**
Woodside Junior School, Amersham

# Lavaball

Lavaball, my fireball pet,
Where should we go today?
Up a mountain?
Down a volcano?
Or perhaps we surf a wave?

Lavaball, my fireball pet,
All the adventures we could have,
Through a portal?
See the future?
*Whoosh!*

Lavaball, my fireball pet,
You light up their wonderland indeed.
You know you're my BFF!
Maybe you decide...
Where we will be tomorrow?

**Dixie Ferguson (9)**
Woodside Junior School, Amersham

# Talking To Aliens

The freaky aliens came out of space.
I was scared of his face.
I didn't know what it was,
And I said, "Soz."
I had never seen an alien before,
One had never knocked on my front door.
I said, "Hello," and it said, "Blah, blah, blah!"
"How old are you?" He said, "Eek, blur, plah!"

**Becky Kemp (7)**
Woodside Junior School, Amersham

# Cookie Nightmare

Chocolate Cookie has cookie problems
Like sugar rush, so many problems.
Cookies oh cookies
We stare, you're so lucky
Your nightmare circle cookie
Look in a bookie
To see a cookie
Cookies are so yummy
And just so crummy
Ask your own mummy
To be more yummy
For my little tummy!

**Lehna Kaur Bains (9)**
Woodside Junior School, Amersham

# Flying Food

Suddenly, through my door,
I saw scrumptious food soar.

There were hot hot dogs,
And delicious chocolate logs.

As I glanced up at the sky,
I saw food fly by.

Out of the air, I take
A beautifully decorated cake.

Can I have more?
I've just had four.

**Molly Meehan (7)**
Woodside Junior School, Amersham

# Unicorn Land

I wish I was a unicorn with flowers in my hair.
I'd dance around the fire
Spreading magical dreams everywhere.
Happiness, joy, and magic
Would spin around me in the air,
Oh, I wish I was a unicorn with flowers in my hair.
Have a bright rainbow day
While the unicorns dance and play.

**Elasia Kate Jbilou (7)**
Woodside Junior School, Amersham

# Young Writers Information

We hope you have enjoyed reading this book – and that you will continue to in the coming years.

If you're a young writer who enjoys reading and creative writing, or the parent of an enthusiastic poet or story writer, do visit our website www.youngwriters.co.uk. Here you will find free competitions, workshops and games, as well as recommended reads, a poetry glossary and our blog. There's lots to keep budding writers motivated to write!

If you would like to order further copies of this book, or any of our other titles, then please give us a call or visit www.youngwriters.co.uk.

Young Writers
Remus House
Coltsfoot Drive
Peterborough
PE2 9BF
(01733) 890066
info@youngwriters.co.uk

Join in the conversation!
Tips, news, giveaways and much more!

**f** YoungWritersUK   **🐦** @YoungWritersCW